Prepare the Way for the Lord
Leader Guide

PREPARE THE WAY FOR THE LORD
ADVENT AND THE MESSAGE OF JOHN THE BAPTIST

978-1-7910-2348-5 *Hardcover*
978-1-7910-2349-2 *eBook*
978-1-7910-235-08 *Large Print*

DVD
978-1-7910-2353-9

Leader Guide
978-1-7910-2351-5
978-1-7910-2352-2 *eBook*

Download a free children's leader guide and youth study at AdamHamilton.com/ PrepareTheWay

Also by Adam Hamilton

24 Hours That Changed the World	*Half Truths*	*Simon Peter*
Christianity and World Religions	*Incarnation*	*Speaking Well*
	John	*The Call*
Christianity's Family Tree	*Leading Beond the Walls*	*The Journey*
Confronting the Controversies	*Living Unafraid*	*The Lord's Prayer*
	Love to Stay	*The Walk*
Creed	*Making Sense of the Bible*	*The Way*
Enough	*Moses*	*Unfraid*
Faithful	*Not a Silent Night*	*When Christians Get It Wrong*
Final Words from the Cross	*Revival*	
	Seeing Gray in a World of Black and White	*Words of Life*
Forgiveness		*Why?*

For more information, visit AdamHamilton.com.

ADAM HAMILTON

Author of *Creed*, *The Walk*, and *The Journey*

PREPARE THE WAY FOR THE LORD

ADVENT

AND THE MESSAGE OF JOHN THE BAPTIST

LEADER GUIDE

BY MIKE POTEET

Abingdon Press | Nashville

Prepare the Way for the Lord
Advent and the Message of John the Baptist
Leader Guide

Copyright © 2022 Abingdon Press
All rights reserved.

978-1-7910-2351-5

Scripture quotations unless noted otherwise are from the Common English Bible. Copyright © 2011 by the Common English Bible. All rights reserved. Used by permission. http://www.CommonEnglishBible.com.

Cover Image: Piero della Francesca (1415-1492), *The Baptism of Christ*, after 1437, egg on poplar, 167 × 116 cm, National Gallery, London, https://www.nationalgallery.org.uk/paintings/piero-della-francesca-the-baptism-of-christ. John's baptism of Jesus in the River Jordan is the pivotal moment when the lives of Jesus and his cousin John intersect. The scene is bathed in light from above, with light, pastel colors, and shadows that create depth. Italian Renaissance artist Piero della Francesca is known for his use of geometry and perspective, which he uses here to highlight the figure of Jesus.

MANUFACTURED IN THE UNITED STATES OF AMERICA

CONTENTS

CONTENTS

INTRODUCTION

In his book *Prepare the Way for the Lord*, Adam Hamilton, senior pastor of the United Methodist Church of the Resurrection in Leawood, Kansas, invites readers to consider the birth, life, ministry, death, and continuing significance of John the Baptist. As Hamilton explains, like a herald sent in antiquity to announce the visit of royalty, John the Baptist was sent to announce the coming of Jesus Christ, as recounted in all four New Testament Gospels.

The season of Advent, the four Sundays before Christmas, is the Christian liturgical season characterized by preparation for Christ's coming: his first coming as an infant, his second coming at the end of time, and his coming here and now through his Spirit into the world and into believers' hearts. As such, traditional Advent readings, such as those in the Revised Common Lectionary, feature John the Baptist prominently. "No other figure in scripture," writes Hamilton, "is more closely associated with this idea of preparation, of making people ready for the coming of Christ, than John the Baptist."

This Leader Guide is for adults leading groups in a congregational setting who are studying *Prepare the Way for the Lord*. While it is ideally suited as an Advent study, it can be used, with minor adaptations, at other times of year as well. Leaders will want to read *Prepare the Way for the Lord* in order to lead this study most effectively. They should also encourage participants to read Hamilton's book, although participants may also get value out of the study on its own.

Each session in this Leader Guide covers one chapter from Hamilton's book, in two or three segments of discussion questions. You likely will not have time to use all the questions provided. Choose those most interesting and relevant to your group.

Don't be afraid to follow as the Spirit leads, but keep the session's objectives in mind lest your group finds itself pursuing irrelevant and confusing lines of discussion.

Please note that leaders should always be prepared to answer first any question they ask, to model and encourage willing participation. These sessions are not designed to work without people who are willing to talk—as leader, you must be ready to go first!

In addition to the discussion questions at the heart of each session, these session plans include:

- **Session Objectives** to keep in mind while planning your session. If one or more objectives do not seem to suit your group, for whatever reason, feel free to focus on the more appropriate objectives. The suggested objectives arise naturally out of the scriptures Hamilton discusses in his book.
- **Biblical Foundations** are key Bible passages, presented for the leader's ready reference. Some sessions will refer to other scriptures as well, but these passages are ones with which leaders should be most familiar before each session.
- **Before Your Session** includes steps to help you prepare before your gathering. Be sure to attend to these preparations before each session. Most sessions involve little to no preparation beyond reading and thinking about the material beforehand, but some suggest optional preparations requiring extra time or materials. In addition, be sure to review the guidelines for leading virtual or hybrid meetings, found below.
- **Starting Your Session** welcomes your group and introduces the main ideas. This section includes suggestions

for "priming the pump" for discussion, and a suggested Opening Prayer.

- **Watch the Video.** If you are using the DVD companion to Hamilton's book or plan to stream the videos via Amplify Media, this section will give you discussion questions specific to each segment. You can and should also invite general responses to each video segment.

- **Closing Your Session** leads you through the end of your gathering. This section suggests a closing discussion and activity as well as a Closing Prayer.

- **Sing Together (optional).** For groups that enjoy singing together (or who are willing to do so during the holidays), each session suggests a thematically appropriate hymn.

- **Optional Extensions** contain ideas for further research and activities individuals or the whole group can pursue beyond the sessions themselves.

Thank you for being willing to lead your group in studying *Prepare the Way for the Lord.* May the Holy Spirit prepare you and all who participate for a more meaningful celebration of Christmas—and, even more importantly, for a more committed life as one who, like John, witnesses to Jesus Christ—through the experience!

ADAPTING FOR VIRTUAL SMALL GROUP SESSIONS

Meeting online is a great option for a number of situations. During a time of a public-health hazard, such as the COVID-19 pandemic, online meetings are a welcome opportunity for people to converse while seeing each other's faces. Online meetings can also expand the "neighborhood" of possible group members, because people can log in from just about anywhere in the world. This also gives those who do not have access to transportation or who prefer not to travel at certain times of day the chance to participate.

The guidelines below will help you lead an effective and enriching group study using an online videoconferencing platform such as Zoom, Webex, Google Meet, Microsoft Teams, or another virtual meeting platform of your choice.

BASIC FEATURES FOR VIRTUAL MEETINGS

There are many choices for videoconferencing platforms. You may have personal experience and comfort using a particular service, or your church may have a subscription that will influence your choice.

Whichever option you choose, it is recommended that you use a platform that supports the following features:

- **Synchronous Video and Audio:** Your participants can see and speak to each other live, in real time. Participants have the ability to turn their video off and on, and to mute and unmute their audio.
- **Chat:** Your participants can send text messages to the whole group or individuals from within the virtual meeting. Participants can put active hyperlinks (for example, "clickable" internet addresses) into the chat for other participants' convenience.
- **Screen Sharing:** Participants can share the contents of their screen with other participants (the meeting host's permission may be required).
- **Video Sharing:** Participants (or the host) can share videos and computer audio via screen share, so that all participants can view the videos each week.
- **Breakout Rooms:** Meeting hosts can automatically or manually send participants into virtual smaller groups and can determine whether the rooms end automatically after a set period of time. Hosts can communicate with all breakout rooms. *This feature is useful if your group is large, or if you wish to break into smaller teams of two or three for certain activities. If you have a smaller group, this feature may not be necessary.*

Check with your pastor or director of discipleship to see if your church has a preferred platform or an account with one or more of these platforms that you might use. In most instances, only the host will need to be signed in to the account; others can participate without being registered.

Zoom, Webex, Google Meet, and Microsoft Teams all offer free versions of their platform, which you can use if your church doesn't have an account. However, there may be some restrictions (for instance, Zoom's free version limits meetings to forty-five minutes). Check each platform's website to be sure you are aware of any such restrictions before you sign up.

Once you have selected a platform, familiarize yourself with all of its features and controls so that you can facilitate virtual meetings comfortably. The platform's website will have lists of features and helpful tutorials, often third-party sites will have useful information or instructions as well.

There are additional features on many that help play your video more effectively. In Zoom, for example, as you click the "share screen" option and see the screen showing your different windows, check at the bottom of that window to choose "optimize for video clips" and "share audio." These ensure that your group hears the audio and that, when using a clip, the video resolution is compressed to fit the bandwidth that you have.

In addition to videoconferencing software, it is also advisable to have access to slide-creation software such as Microsoft PowerPoint or Google Slides. These can be used to prepare easy slides for screen-sharing to display discussion questions, quotes from the study book, or scripture passages. If you don't have easy access to these, you can create a document and share it—but make sure the print size is easy to read.

VIDEO SHARING

For a video-based study, it's important to be able to screen-share your videos so that all participants can view them in your study session. The good news is, whether you have the videos on DVD or streaming files, it is possible to play them in your session.

All of the videoconferencing platforms mentioned above support screen-sharing videos. Some have specific requirements for assuring that sound will play clearly in addition to the videos. Follow your videoconferencing platform instructions carefully, and test the video sharing in advance to be sure it works.

If you wish to screen-share a DVD video, you may need to use a different media player. Some media players will not allow you to share your screen when you play copyright-protected DVDs. VLC is a free media player that is safe and easy to use. To try this software, download at videolan.org/VLC.

What about copyright? DVDs like those you use for group study are meant to be used in a group setting "real time." That is, whether you meet in person, online, or in a hybrid setting, Abingdon Press encourages use of your DVD or streaming video.

What is allowed: Streaming an Abingdon DVD over Zoom, Teams, or similar platform during a small group session.

What is not allowed: Posting video of a published DVD study to social media or YouTube for later viewing.

If you have any questions about permissions and copyright, email permissions@abingdonpress.com.

Amplify Media. The streaming subscription platform Amplify Media makes it easy to share streaming videos for groups. When your church has an Amplify subscription, your group members can sign on and have access to the video sessions. With access, they may watch the video on their own ahead of your group meeting, watch the streaming video during your group meeting, or view it again after the meeting. Thousands of videos are on AmplifyMedia.com making it easy to watch anytime, anywhere, and on any device from phones and tablets to Smart TVs and desktops.

Visit AmplifyMedia.com to learn more or call 1-800-672-1789, option 4, to hear about the current offers.

COMMUNICATING WITH YOUR GROUP

Clear communication with your small group before and throughout your study is crucial no matter how you meet, but it is doubly important if you are gathering virtually.

Advertising the Study. Be sure to advertise your virtual study on your church's website and/or in its newsletter, as well as any social media that your church uses. Request pastors or other worship leaders to announce it in worship services.

Registration. Encourage people to register for the online study so that you can know all participants and have a way to contact them. Ideally, you will collect an email address for each participant so that you can send them communications and links to your virtual meeting sessions. An event planning tool such as SignUpGenius makes this easy and gives you a database of participants and their email addresses.

Welcome Email. Before your first session, several days in advance, send an email to everyone who has registered for the study, welcoming them to the group, reminding them of the date and time of your first meeting, and including a link to join the virtual meeting. It's also a good idea to include one or two discussion questions to "prime the pump" for reflection and conversation when you gather.

If you have members without internet service, or if they are uncomfortable using a computer and videoconferencing software, let them know they may telephone into the meeting. Provide them the number and let them know that there is usually a unique phone number for each meeting.

Weekly Emails. Send a new email two or three days before each week's session, again including the link to join your virtual meeting and one or two discussion questions to set the stage for discussion. Feel free to use any of the questions in the Leader Guide for this purpose. If you find a particular quote from the book that is especially meaningful, include this as well.

Facebook. Consider creating a private Facebook group for your small group, where you can hold discussion and invite reflection between your weekly meetings. Each week, post one or two quotes from the study book along with a short question for reflection, and invite people to respond in the comments. These questions can come straight from the Leader Guide, and you can revisit the Facebook conversation during your virtual meeting.

You might also consider posting these quotes and questions on your church's main Facebook page, inviting people in your congregation to join the conversation beyond your small group. This can be a great way to involve others in your study, or to let people know about it and invite them to join your next virtual meeting.

DURING YOUR VIRTUAL SESSIONS

During your virtual sessions, follow these tips to be sure you are prepared and that everything runs as smoothly as possible.

Getting Ready

- Familiarize yourself with the controls and features of your videoconferencing platform, using instructions or tutorials available via the platform's website or third-party sites.
- Be sure you are leading the session from a well-lit place in front of a background free from excessive distractions.
- As leader, log into the virtual meeting early. You want to be a good host who is present to welcome participants by name as they arrive. This also gives you time to check how you appear on camera, so that you can make any last-minute adjustments to your lighting and background if needed.

Creating Community Online

- During each session, pay attention to who is speaking and who is not. Because of video and audio lags as well as internet connections of varying quality, some participants may inadvertently speak over each other without realizing they are doing so. As needed, directly prompt specific people to speak if they wish (for example, "Alan, it looked like you were about to say something when Sarah was speaking").
- If your group is especially large, you may want to agree with members on a procedure for being recognized to speak (for example, participants might "raise hands" digitally or type "call on me" in the chat feature).
- Instruct participants to keep their microphones muted during the meeting, so extraneous noise from their location

does not interrupt the meeting. This includes chewing or yawning sounds, which can be embarrassing! When it is time for discussion, participants can unmute themselves.

- Remember some participants may wish to simply observe and listen—do not pressure anyone to speak who does not wish to.
- Always get your group's permission before recording your online sessions. While those who are unable to attend the meeting may appreciate the chance to view it later, respect the privacy of your participants.
- Communicate with your group in between sessions with weekly emails and Facebook posts to spark ongoing discussion.

In challenging times, modern technology has powerful potential to bring God's people together in new and nourishing ways. May such be your experience during this virtual study.

HELP, SUPPORT, AND TUTORIALS

The creators of the most popular virtual meeting platforms have excellent, free resources available online to help you get started using their platform, which teach you everything from how to join a meeting as a participant to how to use the more advanced features like video sharing and breakout rooms. Most of them offer clear written instructions as well as video tutorials and also provide a way to contact the company in case you need additional assistance.

Below are links for five platforms: Zoom, Microsoft Teams, Webex, Google Meet, and GoTo Meeting. If you are using a different platform, go to their website and look for the "Help" or "Resources" page.

Zoom Help Center: https://support.zoom.us/hc/en-us

Contains a comprehensive collection of resources to help you use the Zoom platform, including quick start guides, video tutorials, articles, and specific sets of instructions on various topics and issues.

Microsoft Teams Help & Learning:
https://support.microsoft.com/en-us/teams

A collection of articles, videos, and instructions on how to use the Microsoft Teams platform. Teams offers a number of features. You are most likely to find the help you need for group meetings by navigating to the "Meetings" page, or by clicking "Microsoft Teams training" under "Explore Microsoft Teams."

Webex Help Center: https://help.webex.com/en-us/

Contains articles, videos, and other resources to help you use the Webex platform, with everything from joining the meeting to screen-sharing and using a virtual whiteboard.

Google Meet Help: https://support.google.com/meet/

Contains a list of support topics to help you use the Google Meet platform, in an easy-to-read expandable list that makes it easy to find just what you need.

GoTo Meeting Support: https://support.goto.com/meeting

Here you'll find links with instructions on various topics to help you use the GoTo Meeting platform.

General How-To

In addition to these official support pages, there are numerous independent sites online with clear instructions on using multiple platforms. Here is one excellent resource:

Nerds Chalk: https://nerdschalk.com/

This site is easily searchable and contains numerous articles and how-go guides, with clear titles to help you find exactly what you need. Simply search for your chosen platform and/or what you are trying to accomplish, such as "Breakout rooms" or "Zoom screen share," and navigate to the most relevant link.

SESSION

1

THE ANNUNCIATION: GOD HAS HEARD YOUR PRAYERS

SESSION OBJECTIVES

Through this session's readings, discussion, and activities, participants will:

- Share their current knowledge of and ideas about John the Baptist.
- Appreciate why the Christian church has traditionally remembered John especially during the Advent season.
- Reflect on Elizabeth's and Zechariah's childlessness in the context of biblical and modern ideas about infertility.
- Think about when, why, and how God answers prayer, and examine their own assumptions about prayer in light of these reflections.
- Identify ways in which older adults are called to serve God today.
- Offer specific and concrete images of what "turning back to one another" looks like today.

BIBLICAL FOUNDATIONS

Look, I am sending Elijah the prophet to you,
*   before the great and terrifying day of the LORD arrives.*
Turn the hearts of the parents to the children
*   and the hearts of the children to their parents.*
*   Otherwise, I will come and strike the land with*
*   a curse.*

—*Malachi 4:5-6*

During the rule of King Herod of Judea there was a priest named Zechariah who belonged to the priestly division of Abijah. His wife Elizabeth was a descendant of Aaron. They were both righteous before God, blameless in their observance of all the Lord's commandments and regulations. They had no children because Elizabeth was unable to become pregnant and they both were very old. One day Zechariah was serving as a priest before God because his priestly division was on duty. Following the customs of priestly service, he was chosen by lottery to go into the Lord's sanctuary and burn incense. All the people who gathered to worship were praying outside during this hour of incense offering. An angel from the Lord appeared to him, standing to the right of the altar of incense. When Zechariah saw the angel, he was startled and overcome with fear.

The angel said, "Don't be afraid, Zechariah. Your prayers have been heard. Your wife Elizabeth will give birth to your son and you must name him John. He will be a joy and delight to you, and many people will rejoice at his birth, for he will be great in the Lord's eyes. He must not drink wine and liquor. He will be filled with the Holy Spirit even before his birth. He will bring many Israelites back to the Lord their God. He will go forth before the

*Lord, equipped with the spirit and power of Elijah. He
will turn the hearts of fathers back to their children, and
he will turn the disobedient to righteous patterns of thinking. He will make ready a people prepared for the Lord."*

—Luke 1:5-17

BEFORE YOUR SESSION

- Carefully read the introduction and chapter 1 of *Prepare
  the Way for the Lord*, noting topics about which you have
  questions or want to do further research.
- Read this session's Biblical Foundations several times, as
  well as background information about it from a trusted
  study Bible or commentary.
- You will need: Bibles for participants and/or on-screen
  slides, prepared with scripture texts, to share; newsprint or
  a markerboard, and markers.
- Preview the session 1 video segment and makes notes
  to facilitate your group's discussion of it. Test your
  audiovisual equipment and/or ability to share your
  videoconferencing screen.
- *Optional:* Gather images of John the Baptist to display
  in your session and/or share via your videoconferencing
  screen. Select images from a variety of times and places,
  and in a variety of styles.
- *Optional:* Gather magazines and newspapers for the
  closing discussion.

STARTING YOUR SESSION

Welcome participants and tell them why you are excited about
studying *Prepare the Way for the Lord* with them. Invite participants to
talk briefly about why they are interested in this study and what they
would like to gain from it.

- Adam Hamilton begins his book by sharing memories of anticipating and preparing for the birth of one of his daughters. What memories can you share about preparing for the arrival of a child, your own or someone else's? How are these experiences like and unlike preparing to celebrate the birth of Jesus Christ?

- How does your congregation observe Advent? How do you observe it personally or in your family? Do your Advent observances focus more on celebrating Jesus's first "advent" (coming, arrival, or presence) as a baby, or his second advent "at the climax of human history, or when he returns for us at our death"? Why?

- Traditionally, the Christian church especially remembers John the Baptist during Advent because he was the messenger whose mission was "making people ready for the coming of Christ." What do you know about John the Baptist? What questions, if any, have you had about him? *(Write down participants' questions on newsprint or markerboard so the group can refer back to them during the study.)*

- *If you have gathered images of John the Baptist, share them and ask:* Which of these images of John appeals to you the most? The least? Why? How do you picture John in your imagination?

- What do you think it means to "prepare the way for the Lord" today?

Read this prayer, or one of your own, aloud:

Holy God, who was and is and is to come: As we prepare to celebrate your Son's birth in Bethlehem, keep us mindful of your call to prepare for his future coming and to stay alert for his presence among and within us today. By your Spirit, may you use our study this season of John the Baptist's life, work, and witness to Jesus to make us more ready to prepare Christ's way in the world and in our lives. Amen.

WATCH THE VIDEO

Watch the session 1 segment of the companion video via your DVD player or Amplify Media. Invite responses and comments. Discuss:

- What strikes you as most significant about the historical context into which John the Baptist was born, as Adam Hamilton describes it?
- Hamilton describes Ein Karem and says Christian tradition associates it with John's birth. How important is it to mark places connected to biblical people and events? How, if at all, do you mark places important in the story of your own experience with God?
- If someone wanted to visit a place important to the beginning of your life story, where would you want them to go, and why?
- Hamilton says that just because we don't see the miraculous intervention we may pray for, that does not mean God has not heard us or that God doesn't have compassion for us. Do you agree? Why or why not?

MEETING ELIZABETH AND ZECHARIAH

Recruit a volunteer to read aloud Luke 1:5-7, while others read along silently. Discuss:

- What do we know or what can we infer about Zechariah and Elizabeth from Luke's introduction of them (verses 5-6)?
- Why does this couple have no children (verse 7)?
- "In the ancient world," writes Hamilton, "everyone was expected to have offspring" (p. 7). In your experience, what are society's expectations about having children today? How differently do you think women and men experience social expectations about having children?
- "In the biblical world," writes Hamilton, "the physical causes of infertility were not understood, leaving many

to believe that God was the one who opened or closed a woman's womb" (p. 8). As he notes, some Christians hold this view today, while others don't. Do you believe God wills or causes infertility? Why or why not?

- Hamilton states that God eventually intervened in Elizabeth's and Zechariah's infertility. "When God looked for a woman to bear this messenger, God remembered the prayers of Zechariah and Elizabeth and chose them for this important role in God's redemptive plans" (p. 16). How much comfort and encouragement do you think the Bible's stories about infertile couples offer to infertile couples today? Why? How does or how could your congregation minister to women and couples who want to have children but find themselves unable to have them?

Thinking About Prayers, Answered and Unanswered

Recruit a volunteer to read aloud Luke 1:8-13, while others read along silently. Discuss:

- How might the fact that, as Hamilton notes, "entering the sanctuary [in the Temple] to offer incense... might happen once in a priest's lifetime" (p. 11) help set the stage for the rest of this story?
- Why do you imagine Zechariah felt fear when he saw the angel (verse 12)?
- When, if ever, have you felt "overcome" with a strong emotion (not necessarily fear, as Zechariah felt) while worshipping and praying? To what degree has that experience shaped your ongoing prayer and worship?
- "I wonder," asks Hamilton, "if there are things you have prayed for a long time . . . but have seen no answer?" (p. 13). How do you respond? If there are, which of these

things (if any) would you be willing to talk about with the group?

- Hamilton says prayer is less about asking God for things and more about connecting with God. Do you agree? Why or why not?
- Hamilton tells his congregation "it's okay to pray for the 'grand-slam, out-of-the-park' kind of miracles," but says "God's primary way of working in our world is not... miraculous intervention" (p. 14). Have you ever prayed for a miracle? What happened? Would you encourage people to pray for miracles? Why or why not?
- What does Hamilton mean when he says some people think about God as "the genie in our bottle," (p. 15) and why does he discourage this image of God? Do you think it's easier to recognize others thinking about God this way than it is ourselves? Why or why not?
- "The miracles God works," writes Hamilton, "sometimes come in ways that are different from what we had imagined when we pray" (p. 21). What "miracles" in this sense can you point to, in your own or in others' experience?
- "We are not asking [in prayer] to be delivered from the realities of the human experience," writes Hamilton, "but to invite God to walk with us as our companion, our deliverer, our Lord" (p. 15). When, if ever, is it appropriate to pray for physical deliverance from life's difficult realities—sickness, poverty, oppression, and more? How, if at all, should Christians pray for God to deliver other people in this way? How can prayers for deliverance move us to work for deliverance?
- "God is never offended by our honestly sharing our hopes and desires" (p. 16), writes Hamilton. How do or how could you keep yourself praying to God with honesty and without fear?

- Hamilton writes, "most of the painful things I've ever experienced, the things I wished God would have just miraculously taken away, are the very things that most profoundly shaped my life and made me who I am today" (p. 18). How much or how little can you relate to Hamilton's statement, and why?
- What would you say to someone who asked you, "Why isn't God answering my prayers?"

AFFIRMING GOD'S CHOICE OF THOSE WHO ARE "VERY OLD"

Discuss:

- Commenting on Elizabeth's and Zechariah's advanced age, Hamilton writes "the point Luke makes here is a point made throughout scripture, that God often chooses and uses older adults to do God's greatest work" (p. 23). What Bible stories about God using older adults can you remember? Which of these stories, if any, have had particular meaning for you, and why?
- While Zechariah was called to continue his priestly service, Hamilton calls Zechariah's role as John the Baptist's father "his greatest adventure yet" (p. 24). Who do you know or know of who has had their greatest adventure, or discerned their greatest calling, late in life? Why does it take some people a long time to discern their greatest calling?
- What older adults have you known through whom you would say God was or is at work, and how?
- What does or could your congregation do to encourage older adults to see themselves as those who "never retire from God's work?" (p. 26).

Closing Your Session: Being a People Prepared for the Lord

Recruit volunteers to read aloud Malachi 4:5-6 (or the entire chapter), while others read along silently. Read aloud from *Prepare the Way for the Lord*: "The angel Gabriel makes clear [to Zechariah] that John is coming to be the Elijah that Malachi had spoken of more than four hundred years earlier. And for us, today, as in Malachi's day and John's day… being prepared for the Lord involves turning back to one another, turning back to right ways of thinking" (p. 29). Discuss:

- Why does Malachi say "the day of the Lord" will be "great and terrifying" (see also 4:1-3)? How do you react to the prophet's words?
- From what you know of John the Baptist, what did he do to fulfill Malachi's prophecy?
- What does or what would turning people's hearts back to one another look like, practically and concretely, in society today? in your community? in your congregation? in your own family?

Optional: Distribute magazines and newspapers. Invite participants to look through them, and/or to search online, for images they believe illustrate people "turning back to one another." Invite volunteers to talk briefly about the image(s) they choose.

Read this prayer, or one of your own, aloud:

God of the future, you have never failed to call your people back to righteous living. We praise you for messengers in the past who have borne faithful witness to you and dare to pray you would make us people who prepare your way in our own time, for the sake of him whose coming John the Baptist proclaimed, our Lord Jesus Christ. Amen.

SING TOGETHER (OPTIONAL)

Reflecting on prayer as a way to experience communion with God in difficult times, Hamilton mentions "Precious Lord, Take My Hand" by Thomas Dorsey (1938; https://hymnary.org/text/precious_lord _take_my_hand). Sing or read aloud together this hymn's lyrics as your closing prayer.

OPTIONAL EXTENSIONS

- Read some of the biblical stories of childless women and couples that Hamilton mentions: Abraham and Sarah (Genesis 16:1-6; 17:15-21; 18:1-15; 21:1-7); Isaac and Rebekah (Genesis 25:21-26); Samson's parents (Judges 13); and Hannah and Elkanah (1 Samuel 1). How are these stories like and unlike the story of Elizabeth and Zechariah? How might God speak through these stories to couples and women struggling with infertility today?
- Listen as a group to Garth Brooks's song "Unanswered Prayers" (1990). Hamilton writes, "Like the song says, I thank God for unanswered prayers" (p. 18). What does Hamilton mean? Do you agree with Brooks's sentiment? Why or why not? If you were to write a song about an unanswered prayer in your own life, what would that song say and sound like?

SESSION
2

PREGNANCY, BIRTH, CIRCUMCISION, AND ZECHARIAH'S PROPHECY

SESSION OBJECTIVES

Through this session's readings, discussion, and activities, participants will:

- Ponder how asking questions and taking time for silence can nurture faith.
- Examine Elizabeth and Mary's relationship as a model for supportive and celebrative networks of caring that bring younger and older people together.
- Reflect on Zechariah's praise of God's grace in Luke 1:68-79 for its insights into God's character, and God's activity through John the Baptist and Jesus.
- Identify specific ways they can reflect God's light to those "sitting in darkness" this Advent season.

29

BIBLICAL FOUNDATIONS

Zechariah said to the angel, "How can I be sure of this? My wife and I are very old."

The angel replied, "I am Gabriel. I stand in God's presence. I was sent to speak to you and to bring this good news to you. Know this: What I have spoken will come true at the proper time. But because you didn't believe, you will remain silent, unable to speak until the day when these things happen."

Meanwhile, the people were waiting for Zechariah, and they wondered why he was in the sanctuary for such a long time. When he came out, he was unable to speak to them. They realized he had seen a vision in the temple, for he gestured to them and couldn't speak.

—Luke 1:18-22

[Mary] entered Zechariah's home and greeted Elizabeth. When Elizabeth heard Mary's greeting, the child leaped in her womb, and Elizabeth was filled with the Holy Spirit. With a loud voice she blurted out, "God has blessed you above all women, and he has blessed the child you carry. Why do I have this honor, that the mother of my Lord should come to me? As soon as I heard your greeting, the baby in my womb jumped for joy. Happy is she who believed that the Lord would fulfill the promises he made to her."

—Luke 1:40-45

When the time came for Elizabeth to have her child, she gave birth to a boy. Her neighbors and relatives celebrated with her because they had heard that the Lord had shown her great mercy. On the eighth day, it came time to circumcise the child. They wanted to name him Zechariah because that was his father's name. But his mother replied, "No, his name will be John."

*They said to her, "None of your relatives have that name."
Then they began gesturing to his father to see what he
wanted to call him.*

*After asking for a tablet, he surprised everyone by writing,
"His name is John." At that moment, Zechariah was able
to speak again, and he began praising God.*

—Luke 1:57-64

*"Bless the Lord God of Israel
     because he has come to help and has delivered his
     people....*
*You, child, will be called a prophet of the Most High,
     for you will go before the Lord to prepare his way.*
*You will tell his people how to be saved
     through the forgiveness of their sins.*
*Because of our God's deep compassion,
     the dawn from heaven will break upon us,
     to give light to those who are sitting in darkness
     and in the shadow of death,
          to guide us on the path of peace."*

—Luke 1:68, 76-79

BEFORE YOUR SESSION

- Carefully read chapter 2 of *Prepare the Way for the Lord*, noting topics about which you have questions or want to do further research.
- Read this session's Biblical Foundations several times, as well as background information about it from a trusted study Bible or commentary.
- You will need: Bibles for participants and/or on-screen slides prepared with the scripture texts to share. *Optional*: Prepare a handout and/or screen slides your group can use to read Luke 1:68-79 together, from the same translation.

- If you plan to view the companion video, preview the session 2 segment and make notes to facilitate your group's discussion of it. Test your audiovisual equipment and/or ability to share your videoconferencing screen.

STARTING YOUR SESSION

Welcome participants. Tell them you would like them to keep a period of silence. You will watch a stopwatch or clock; encourage them to avoid looking at any timekeeping device or to mentally count the seconds. Announce the start of the silence. At ninety seconds, announce the silence's end. Discuss:

- How long do you think we kept silent?
- What did you think as we kept silence? What sensations did you notice, within or around you?
- How easy, in general, do you find it to keep silent? Why?
- When and how does our society value silence? When does it not?

Tell participants this session moves from silence to speech in events surrounding the birth of John the Baptist.

Read this prayer, or one of your own, aloud:

Before you, Holy God, we sometimes fall silent in humility and awe. At other times, we cannot help but shout and sing your praise. In this time of study, help us listen—in the scripture, in our discussions with each other, and in our hearts—for your Word, that we may learn how to more faithfully echo and embody it, for the sake of Jesus Christ, your Word made flesh. Amen.

WATCH THE VIDEO

Watch the session 2 segment of the companion DVD. Invite responses and comments. Discuss:

- Adam Hamilton says that most key decisions in our lives require a leap of faith. Do you agree? Why or why not?
- Why was Wendell Lady important for Hamilton? Who has been like Wendell Lady for you—investing in *your* life, and finding meaning and joy in walking alongside *you*?
- Hamilton mentions the bronze statue of Elizabeth and Mary at the Church of the Visitation at Ein Karem. In his book he says he found the statue of these two pregnant women "quite beautiful." How much beauty does society today see in women who are pregnant? How much does the church see? Why do you answer as you do?
- Hamilton recalls the buses full of joyful women from Africa and Asia who asked him to take their pictures next to the statue of Elizabeth and Mary. He describes the kinship these women felt with Elizabeth and Mary, whose close relationship echoed the relationships they had with aunts and nieces, cousins and friends. What extended relationships with relatives (by blood, by law, or by choice) have brought or now bring you joy?
- As we'll read, Luke says the Holy Spirit was present and active during Elizabeth and Mary's visit. How often do you think of your family visitations as opportunities for the Spirit to act? Why?

SEARCHING FOR CERTAINTY AND KEEPING SACRED SILENCE

Recruit a volunteer to read aloud Luke 1:18-20, while others read along silently. Discuss:

- What do you think about Zechariah's response to Gabriel's announcement (verse 18)? How is it like or unlike Mary's response to a similar announcement from Gabriel (Luke 1:34)?

- "Our brains were wired for questioning, for critical thinking, and doubts that inevitably arise are meant to lead us to dig deeper, to search for answers," (p. 38) writes Hamilton. "We are meant to ask questions. Sometimes our doubts are well founded" (p. 37). When have your doubts about something or someone led you to discover and avoid trouble? In what other situations can skepticism prove healthy and productive?
- When, if ever, have you or someone you know asked or wanted to ask God, "How can I be sure of this?" What happened?
- Hamilton quotes author and minister Frederick Buechner: "Doubts are the ants in the pants of faith. They keep it awake and moving" (p. 37). What does this quote mean? Do you agree? Why or why not? How, if ever, have doubts led you to deeper faith?
- Hamilton states "there are very few things about which we can be absolutely sure. Most decisions we make require a leap of faith" (p. 38). What "leap of faith" decision in your life do you remember most, and why? Why would or wouldn't you make that decision again?
- Hamilton writes that the longer he lives, the more comfortable he is with uncertainty and simple trust in God. Do you share this experience? Why or why not?
- "While we, like Zechariah, crave certainty, God gives us mystery..." (p. 39). How does or how could your congregation recognize God's gift of mystery—in its worship, in its education ministries, in its service to others, or in other ways—while encouraging people to both trust God and ask God questions?
- If, as Hamilton asserts, Zechariah's question is understandable and God "gives us mystery," do you think of Zechariah's miraculously imposed nine-month silence (verses 20-22) as a "punishment?" If so, why did his

question merit punishment? If not, what was his silence meant to accomplish?

- Hamilton thinks "God was asking Zechariah to talk less and to listen more" (p. 40). When have you found less talking and more listening, whether to God or to other people, the right approach, and why?

- Hamilton shares his experience of hearing the Spirit's whisper during a silent retreat at a monastery. When, if ever, have you heard God speaking to you in and through silence? How? Where do you go when you want or need to take time for silence?

- How does your congregation take time for silence in its worship? Do you think it takes enough? Why or why not?

FINDING CELEBRATION AND SUPPORT IN CARING NETWORKS

Recruit a volunteer to read aloud Luke 1:40-45, while others read along silently. Discuss:

- In the sixth month of Elizabeth's pregnancy, Gabriel tells Mary of Nazareth that Mary will be Jesus's mother (1:26-33). Hamilton asks, "Why did Mary leave her hometown so quickly...to find Elizabeth?" (p. 46). What do you think?

- How does John's jumping for joy in Elizabeth's womb at the presence of Jesus in Mary's womb anticipate John's future relationship to Jesus?

- Hamilton states Elizabeth essentially prophesies in her words to Mary. How so? What do Elizabeth's words show us about the nature and function of prophetic speech? When, if ever, have you heard prophecy for yourself?

- Hamilton points out Elizabeth is the first person to make "the fundamental confession of the Christian faith," that

Jesus is Lord (p. 48; see Luke 1:43 and Romans 10:9).
Who was the first person you heard make this confession?
If you made this confession yourself, when did you first
make it? How can and do Christians make this confession
with more than words?

- "Elizabeth is the first to celebrate Mary's pregnancy,"
  Hamilton notes (p. 50). When and how have you
  celebrated someone's pregnancy?

- Hamilton sees Mary's visit to Elizabeth as evidence of
  a deep relationship that likely formed over many years,
  beginning when Mary was younger. What long-lasting
  relationships with older adults have positively influenced
  you, and how?

- "Everyone needs an Elizabeth," writes Hamilton, "but as
  we grow older, we also find ourselves needing a Mary"
  (p. 53). When and how, if ever, have you mentored,
  encouraged, and celebrated a younger person (whether or
  not that person is your blood or legal relative)?

- How does or how could your congregation celebrate,
  support, and create the "dense networks of caring"
  Hamilton sees in Elizabeth and Mary's relationship?

GIVING VOICE TO GOD'S GRACE

Recruit a volunteer to read aloud Luke 1:57-64, while others read
along silently in their Bibles. Discuss:

- The name "John" (Hebrew, *Johanan*) means "The Lord is
  gracious." How appropriate is and will this name be for
  Elizabeth and Zechariah's child?

- Hamilton notes the Greek word for *grace* appears more
  than 150 times in the New Testament. Christians believe
  grace is a defining characteristic of God (along with other
  attributes like love and justice). How do you define *grace*?

- Hamilton calls receiving and giving grace "the rhythm of the Christian life" (p. 57). What does Ephesians 2:8-10 teach about the rhythm of grace? When was a time you experienced grace? When was a time you extended grace to another person?

Optional: Invite participants to read together (responsively or in unison) Luke 1:67-79, using the handouts and/or slides you prepared before the session. Alternatively, invite volunteers to read aloud Luke 1:67-68, 76-79, while others read along silently. Discuss:

- What word, phrase, or image in Zechariah's prophetic speech most grabs your attention or excites your imagination? Why?
- How do Zechariah's words characterize God? Which of these characteristics do you find most meaningful, and why?
- How is the work Zechariah says God will do through Jesus and John consistent with God's past work for Israel? How is it new and different?
- When, if ever, have you burst out in praise of God's grace, as the Holy Spirit moved Zechariah to do?

CLOSING YOUR SESSION: LIGHT TO THOSE IN DARKNESS

Read aloud from *Prepare the Way for the Lord*: Zechariah's "prophetic word captures the Advent message of John the Baptist. It summarizes what Advent is all about.... This is Advent, when the dawn from heaven breaks upon us, regardless of the darkness we've been living in" (pp. 61, 63).

Ask participants to think about someone they think is "sitting in darkness" (Luke 1:79). Then ask participants to think about at least one specific thing they could and will do this Advent season to reflect God's light for that person. Invite those who wish to share their responses to do so.

Read this prayer, or one of your own, aloud:

Blessed are you, O God, for compassionately shining your light of love on us in Jesus Christ. Although you called your prophet John to go before him in a unique way, you call us to carry his light into darkness even today. By the power of your Spirit, may we serve you without fear and walk always in paths of peace. Amen.

SING TOGETHER (OPTIONAL)

Hamilton mentions "Let All Mortal Flesh Keep Silence," the "oldest hymn in *The United Methodist Hymnal*" (#41)—and possibly many others (https://hymnary.org/text/let_all_mortal_flesh_keep_silence). Sing or read aloud together this hymn's lyrics as the closing prayer.

OPTIONAL EXTENSIONS

- Luke often emphasizes the Holy Spirit's presence and work throughout not only his Gospel but also its "sequel," the Acts of the Apostles. Have participants spend five minutes searching for mentions of the Spirit in Luke and Acts, using print and/or electronic concordances or other search tools. Based on these mentions, what can we say about the Spirit's nature and activity? How does your congregation emphasize the Spirit's presence and work? How do participants do so in their own lives?

- Invite a participant to research the history and significance of the "Hail Mary" prayer, which incorporates Elizabeth's words to Mary (1:42), in the Roman Catholic tradition. Ask those who have experience praying the Hail Mary to talk about its meaning for them.

- Choose at least two musical settings of Luke 1:68-79, the "Benedictus" (after the first word of the text's Latin translation), to play for your group. Compare and contrast them together. How does each help participants understand or appreciate Zechariah's words in new ways?

SESSION

3

JOHN'S MINISTRY AND PREACHING

SESSION OBJECTIVES

Through this session's readings, discussion, and activities, participants will:

- Reflect on the significance of the Jordan River wilderness as the setting for John the Baptist's ministry, as well as his connections to Israel's past.
- Explore possible connections between John and the Essenes, and how these may help us better understand John's ministry.
- Examine John's preaching of repentance, including its practical implications for Christians today.
- Experience an opportunity to practice confession and to renew their baptism.

BIBLICAL FOUNDATIONS

In the fifteenth year of the rule of the emperor Tiberius—
when Pontius Pilate was governor over Judea and Herod
was ruler over Galilee, his brother Philip was ruler

over Ituraea and Trachonitis, and Lysanias was ruler
over Abilene, during the high priesthood of Annas and
Caiaphas—God's word came to John son of Zechariah
in the wilderness. John went throughout the region of the
Jordan River, calling for people to be baptized to show that
they were changing their hearts and lives and wanted God
to forgive their sins. This is just as it was written in the
scroll of the words of Isaiah the prophet,

A voice crying out in the wilderness:
   "Prepare the way for the Lord;
      make his paths straight.
Every valley will be filled,
   and every mountain and hill will be leveled.
The crooked will be made straight
   and the rough places made smooth.
All humanity will see God's salvation."

—Luke 3:1-6

In those days John the Baptist appeared in the desert of
Judea announcing, "Change your hearts and lives! Here
comes the kingdom of heaven!" He was the one of whom
Isaiah the prophet spoke when he said:

The voice of one shouting in the wilderness,
   "Prepare the way for the Lord;
      make his paths straight."

John wore clothes made of camel's hair, with a leather belt
around his waist. He ate locusts and wild honey.

People from Jerusalem, throughout Judea, and all around
the Jordan River came to him. As they confessed their sins,
he baptized them in the Jordan River.

—Matthew 3:1-6

Then John said to the crowds who came to be baptized
by him, "You children of snakes! Who warned you to

escape from the angry judgment that is coming soon?
Produce fruit that shows you have changed your hearts
and lives. And don't even think about saying to yourselves,
Abraham is our father. I tell you that God is able to raise
up Abraham's children from these stones. The ax is already
at the root of the trees. Therefore, every tree that doesn't
produce good fruit will be chopped down and tossed into
the fire."

The crowds asked him, "What then should we do?"

He answered, "Whoever has two shirts must share with
the one who has none, and whoever has food must do
the same."

Even tax collectors came to be baptized. They said to him,
"Teacher, what should we do?"

He replied, "Collect no more than you are authorized to
collect."

Soldiers asked, "What about us? What should we do?"

He answered, "Don't cheat or harass anyone, and be
satisfied with your pay."

—Luke 3:7-14

BEFORE YOUR SESSION

- Carefully read Chapter 3 of *Prepare the Way for the Lord*, noting topics about which you have questions or want to do further research.
- Read this session's Biblical Foundations several times, as well as background information about it from a trusted study Bible or commentary.
- You will need: Bibles for participants and/or on-screen slides prepared with scripture texts to share.

- If you plan to view the companion video, preview the session 3 segment and make notes to facilitate your group's discussion of it. Test your audiovisual equipment and/or ability to share your videoconferencing screen.
- If gathering in person, fill a large bowl with water and place it in your meeting space. If meeting in a hybrid format or virtually, encourage participants not in the room to have a small bowl of water ready for the session's closing activity.
- *Optional:* Contact participants beforehand, inviting them to locate photos and/or mementos of their own or another's baptism to "show and tell" with the group.
- Unless you know for a fact all participants have been baptized, be careful to lead this session's discussions of baptism in ways that do not make those who are not baptized feel excluded or disrespected. Make positive statements about what baptism means for those who have received it—not negative statements about those who have not received it. Encourage any participants who express interest in being baptized to talk with pastoral leadership. Help facilitate such meetings when possible.

STARTING YOUR SESSION

Welcome participants. Ask them to talk briefly about memories they have of their own or another's baptism. If you contacted participants before the session about finding baptismal photos and mementos, invite them to share those at this time. Discuss:

- What baptismal traditions your congregation practices do you find meaningful, and why?
- If someone who is not Christian asked you to explain baptism's significance, what would you tell her or him?
- If you have been baptized, how often and in what circumstances do you remember this fact?

Tell participants this session will explore the meanings of John the Baptist's ministry of baptism and its continued significance for Christians today.

Read this prayer, or one of your own, aloud:

High and Holy God, you sent your servant John into the wilderness to prepare a people for you by baptism. As we study his ministry today, may your Spirit prepare us to bear ever more faithful witness, in word and deed, to him into whose death and resurrection we have been baptized, your Son Jesus Christ. Amen.

WATCH THE VIDEO

Watch the session 3 segment of the companion DVD. Invite responses and comments. Discuss:

- What is significant about Qumran?
- What makes the Dead Sea Scrolls, produced at Qumran, one of the greatest archaeological discoveries in history?
- The Jews who lived at Qumran lived an ascetic life. They practiced strict self-discipline to prepare themselves for the coming messianic age. With what ascetic religious practices are you familiar, from Christian or other traditions? Have you ever found spiritual value in practicing an ascetic discipline yourself?
- In his book, Hamilton expands on the reasons some scholars think John the Baptist once belonged to or was associated with the Essenes. How does this possible connection affect your understanding of him?
- Hamilton describes his friend, author Mike Slaughter, who challenged his congregation to give more to charity at Christmas than they spent on their family. How could you take this idea seriously—and to what extent would doing so transform your Christmas celebrations?

- If you had the opportunity to renew your baptism (or to be baptized, if you are not already baptized) in the Jordan River, would you want to? Why or why not?

HEARING GOD'S WORD IN THE WILDERNESS

Recruit one volunteer to read aloud Luke 3:1-6 and another to read aloud Matthew 3:1-6. Have other participants read along silently. After both readings, discuss:

- How are Luke's and Matthew's introductions of John alike and unalike? What significance do you find in these similarities and differences?
- Why does Luke take such care to date John the Baptist's ministry? (See also Luke 1:1-4.) What point(s) might Luke be making in juxtaposing the names of many figures of political and religious power with the name of John?
- "God's word came to John...in the wilderness" (verse 2). What other Bible stories do you remember that are set in a wilderness or a desert? What associations do the desert or wilderness have in the Bible? How might those associations shape our understanding of John's ministry and message?
- John was not in just any wilderness, but the wilderness around the Jordan River. What is this river's significance in Israel's past? (Consider especially its appearances in Joshua 3 and 2 Kings 2.) How can these associations inform our appreciation of John's significance?
- Hamilton writes that both the Essenes and John "saw themselves fulfilling the words of Isaiah" (p. 73). Read Isaiah 40:1-5. These words were likely first addressed to Jewish exiles in Babylon more than five hundred years before John, as they prepared to return to Israel. How

does Isaiah's wilderness imagery reflect that hope? How do Matthew and Luke apply that imagery to John?

- Where might and do Christians today, two thousand years later, see wildernesses in need of God's transformation—and how can and do we participate in those transformations?
- Matthew mentions John's rough, simple wilderness dress and diet (verse 4; compare Mark 1:6). How does this detail connect John to Elijah (2 Kings 1:8)? Why is this connection important? (Read again Luke 1:17; Malachi 4:5.)

PRODUCING FRUIT WORTHY OF REPENTANCE

Read aloud from *Prepare the Way for the Lord*: "Both John and the Essenes practiced baptism for purification and forgiveness from sin.... [But] the Essenes were an exclusive community that sought to separate themselves from all they considered sinful" (pp. 73-74). As Hamilton notes, John the Baptist proclaimed a different vision.

Recruit a volunteer to read aloud Luke 3:7-14, while others read along silently. Discuss:

- John called people to "repent," which, as Hamilton explains, translates the Greek word *metanoia*, which means "to think differently afterwards" and "seeing things so differently that it leads to a change of heart and ultimately a change of behavior" (p. 79). What do you think about when you hear the call to "repent"? What images or actions do you associate with the word?
- Hamilton explains the Greek word for sin, *hamartia*, is a term borrowed from archery that means to "miss the mark." How helpful to you is this image for sin? Why or why not? What other images for sin, if any, are meaningful for you?
- How does Hamilton suggest John's attitude toward sinners differed from the Essenes' attitude? Do you think

your congregation sees itself more as "a hospital for sinners or an exclusive club for saints"? (p. 75). Why? How do you think an outsider to your congregation would see it, and why?

- Hamilton notes John calls the crowds seeking baptism "children of snakes" in Luke (3:7), an epithet he reserves for religious leaders, Pharisees and Sadducees, in Matthew (3:7). Are there certain temptations that affect committed religious people more than those who are nonreligious?

- "Today," Hamilton notes, "the word *Pharisee* has come to be synonymous with religious hypocrisy" (even though, as he also notes, "there were many Pharisees that were undoubtedly pious and devout") (p. 83). When have you encountered religious hypocrisy in others? In yourself? How did you respond?

- Why might those listening to John preach have appealed to their descent from Abraham, as John suggests (Matthew 3:9; Luke 3:8)? What does John's response tell us about the responsibilities of living as God's chosen people? (See also Exodus 19:5-6; Amos 3:1-2; 1 Peter 2:9.) What might be the equivalent for Christians today of saying, "Abraham is our father"—and what might John say in response?

- What is the "good fruit" John calls on the crowds, the tax collectors, and the soldiers who hear him to produce (Luke 3:10-14)? Why does John focus on actions alone, and not belief? Does John preach "salvation by works" or "works righteousness"—the idea that we can earn salvation by what we do? Why or why not?

- Hamilton notes that "all the fruit of repentance [of which John speaks], the evidence that our hearts are spiritually preparing for the Kingdom and the coming King, have to do with economics and compassion" (p. 86). If you examined your checkbook or bank statements, what evidence of compassion would you find? What about your congregation's annual budget?

- Hamilton writes, "Focusing on giving and sharing and serving… serves as an antidote to the materialism often experienced in the [Advent and Christmas] season, and in the process, brings greater joy" (p. 87). How, if ever, have you experienced this holiday season dynamic in your own life? In your congregation?
- "If twenty-first-century Americans were standing near the Jordan River listening to John preach," asks Hamilton, "what do you think he would say to us?" (p. 81). How would you respond to this question?

Closing Your Session: Repenting Our Sin, Remembering Our Baptism

Read aloud from *Prepare the Way for the Lord*:

> As the water washed over those John baptized, the symbolic value of this was powerful and varied. There was the obvious imagery of being washed, cleansed, and having one's sins carried away. But as with Christian baptism, there was also the imagery of death and resurrection, dying to the old self and being resurrected as a new person. There was the imagery of birth—we are surrounded by water in the womb, and through water we are born into this world. The waters of baptism came to be seen by early Christians as the womb of God. There was liberation implied as those coming to be baptized joined in the act of passing through the waters of the Red Sea as they were liberated from slavery in Egypt, and passed through the Jordan at nearly that same spot where their forebearers entered the Promised Land.
>
> But it was the idea of forgiveness, cleansing and starting anew (changing their minds and hearts) that seemed most clear in John's preaching and the crowd's response….

When Jesus and his followers continued this practice
of baptizing, it came to signify both repentance and
forgiveness, but also much more. (pp. 95-96)

In chapter 3, Hamilton invites readers to write their own prayer of confession. Give participants time to write such a prayer, either in silence or as you play music appropriate to the themes of this session. When participants are finished, invite volunteers who want to do so to read their written prayers aloud.

If you are gathered in person, gather around the large bowl of water. If you are gathering virtually, invite participants to get their small bowls of water ready. Invite participants to touch the water as they feel moved to do so and perhaps to make the sign of the cross on their foreheads as a way of remembering God's promises of grace and forgiveness in baptism.

Read this prayer from *Prepare the Way for the Lord* (p. 101), or one of your own, aloud:

Lord, forgive me, wash me, fill me. I offer myself to you and renew once more the promise made at my baptism. I confess you, Jesus, as my Savior and my Lord. Help me to follow you today and honor you in all that I do. Amen.

SING TOGETHER (OPTIONAL)

To praise God for John's ministry and its ongoing significance, sing or read aloud together a hymn about John such as "On Jordan's Bank the Baptist's Cry" (Charles Coffin, 1736; translated by John Chandler, 1837; https://hymnary.org/text/on_jordans_bank_the_baptists_cry) or "Wild and Lone the Prophet's Voice" (Carl P. Daw, 1989; https://hymnary.org/text/wild_and_lone_the_prophets_voice).

OPTIONAL EXTENSIONS

- Encourage interested participants to research further the Essenes, the Dead Sea Scrolls, and what their connections might have been to John the Baptist, and to report back some of what they find to the group during your fourth and final session.

- "If you are studying this book with a group," writes Hamilton, "invite your pastor to renew the [baptismal] vows of all in your group at one time" (p. 99). If your group is interested, make arrangements for such a celebration of the renewal of the baptismal covenant, perhaps as a part of your congregation's main worship service. Work with worship planners to find a way for members of your group to talk briefly in the service about this study and why participants want to remember their baptism together. Consider inviting others in the congregation to renew their baptismal vows also.

SESSION

4

WITNESSES, TESTIFYING TO THE LIGHT

SESSION OBJECTIVES

Through this session's readings, discussion, and activities, participants will:

- Define the relationship of John the Baptist to Jesus, drawing on several passages from the Gospels.
- Consider the consequences of speaking God's truth to people in positions of power by studying the story of John the Baptist's arrest and execution.
- Reflect on the images connecting John to Jesus in the prologue to John's Gospel (John 1:1-14), and think about not only new images for communicating the same truths but also practical ways of "witnessing to the light."
- Identify individuals they could and will invite to worship or other participation in congregational life.

BIBLICAL FOUNDATIONS

At that time Jesus came from Galilee to the Jordan River so that John would baptize him. John tried to stop him and said, "I need to be baptized by you, yet you come to me?"

Jesus answered, "Allow me to be baptized now. This is necessary to fulfill all righteousness."

So John agreed to baptize Jesus. When Jesus was baptized, he immediately came up out of the water. Heaven was opened to him, and he saw the Spirit of God coming down like a dove and resting on him. A voice from heaven said, "This is my Son whom I dearly love; I find happiness in him."

—Matthew 3:13-17

Herod himself had arranged to have John arrested and put in prison because of Herodias, the wife of Herod's brother Philip. Herod had married her, but John told Herod, "It's against the law for you to marry your brother's wife!" So Herodias had it in for John. She wanted to kill him, but she couldn't. This was because Herod respected John. He regarded him as a righteous and holy person, so he protected him. John's words greatly confused Herod, yet he enjoyed listening to him.

Finally, the time was right. It was on one of Herod's birthdays, when he had prepared a feast for his high-ranking officials and military officers and Galilee's leading residents. Herod's daughter Herodias came in and danced, thrilling Herod and his dinner guests. The king said to the young woman, "Ask me whatever you wish, and I will give it to you." Then he swore to her, "Whatever you ask I will give to you, even as much as half of my kingdom."

*She left the banquet hall and said to her mother, "What
should I ask for?"*

"John the Baptist's head," Herodias replied.

*Hurrying back to the ruler, she made her request: "I want
you to give me John the Baptist's head on a plate, right this
minute." Although the king was upset, because of his solemn
pledge and his guests, he didn't want to refuse her. So he
ordered a guard to bring John's head. The guard went to the
prison, cut off John's head, brought his head on a plate, and
gave it to the young woman, and she gave it to her mother.
When John's disciples heard what had happened, they came
and took his dead body and laid it in a tomb.*

—*Mark 6:17-29*

*In the beginning was the Word
    and the Word was with God
    and the Word was God.
The Word was with God in the beginning.
Everything came into being through the Word,
    and without the Word
    nothing came into being.
What came into being
    through the Word was life,
    and the life was the light for all people.
The light shines in the darkness,
    and the darkness doesn't extinguish the light.*

*A man named John was sent from God. He came as a
witness to testify concerning the light, so that through him
everyone would believe in the light. He himself wasn't the
light, but his mission was to testify concerning the light.*

*The true light that shines on all people
    was coming into the world....*

*The Word became flesh
    and made his home among us.*

> *We have seen his glory,*
> *glory like that of a father's only son,*
> *full of grace and truth.*
>
> —*John 1:1-9, 14*

BEFORE YOUR SESSION

- Carefully read chapter 4 of *Prepare the Way for the Lord,* noting topics about which you have questions or want to do further research.
- Read this session's Biblical Foundations several times, as well as background information about it from a trusted study Bible or commentary.
- You will need: Bibles for participants and/or on-screen slides, prepared with scripture texts to share;.
- You may want to have trusted Bible commentaries for in-person participants' reference.
- If you plan to view the companion video, preview the session 4 segment and make notes to facilitate your group's discussion of it. Test your audiovisual equipment and/or ability to share your videoconferencing screen.

STARTING YOUR SESSION

Welcome participants. Ask volunteers to talk briefly about an important friendship with one of their peers when they were a child. Invite them to talk about how the friendship began, their strongest memory of it, whether it has lasted, and how it has shaped their lives.

Summarize Hamilton's wonderings about the relationship John the Baptist and Jesus shared growing up. Invite participants to respond to Hamilton's wonderings and to add some of their own. Read aloud from *Prepare the Way for the Lord*: "If they [John and Jesus] spent time with one another in their teens and twenties, they surely spent hours discussing scripture, theology, ethics, the coming of the Messiah, and more" (pp. 107-108). Tell participants this session will explore biblical accounts of the relationship between John and Jesus.

Read this prayer, or one of your own, aloud:

Holy God, who was and is and is to come: At the beginning of all things you created light in the darkness, and in the birth of Jesus, your divine light entered this dark world you nevertheless love and have redeemed. As we conclude this study of John, whom you sent to testify to the light, equip us by your Spirit to bear testimony, as well,, never shrinking from your summons to walk in the light of your Son, our Savior, Jesus Christ. Amen.

WATCH THE VIDEO

Watch the session 4 segment of the companion video. Invite responses and comments. Discuss:

- Adam Hamilton describes some of his congregation's Christmas Eve worship traditions. How does your congregation observe Christmas Eve? Which of these Christmas Eve traditions do you find most meaningful, and why?
- How were John the Baptist's and Jesus's ministries different? How were they the same? Why do these similarities and differences matter for Christians today?
- John says of Jesus, "He must increase, and I must decrease." What is remarkable about this attitude of humility? How does John the Baptist encourage you to adopt this attitude in your own life?
- Have you heard or prayed the prayer "More of Thee and less of me" before? What would more of Christ, less of yourself look like, specifically, in your life at this time?
- Hamilton recorded this video during Russia's invasion of Ukraine in 2022. As you study this book, what events

confront you with darkness—and where do you see God's light shining in that darkness? How are or how could you and your congregation witness to God's light in these dark situations?

CLARIFYING THE CONNECTION BETWEEN JOHN AND JESUS

Read aloud from *Prepare the Way for the Lord*: "John knew he was the forerunner, preparing the way for the Messiah. Jesus and John both believed Jesus was that Messiah" (p. 110). Tell participants the Gospels contain several passages making clear the relationship between the two, passages that may reflect historical rivalry between the two men's disciples, and ongoing debate in the earliest Christian traditions about who was more important than whom.

Recruit a volunteer to read aloud Matthew 3:13-17, while other participants read along silently. Discuss:

- "Some have asked why Jesus needed to be baptized at all," writes Hamilton (p. 111). How does this exchange between Jesus and John answer that question?
- What does "fulfilling all righteousness" mean for Jesus?
- What difference does or could it make to you that Jesus was baptized in order to identify with us and with our humanity, as Hamilton suggests?
- What significance do the heavenly voice's words at Jesus's baptism have for Christians who are baptized today?

Form three small groups of participants. Assign each group one of the following scriptures to read and discuss:

- Matthew 11:2-18
- Luke 7:18-35
- John 3:22-36

Ask each small group to determine what its assigned passage claims about the relationship between John and Jesus. (If possible, provide trusted Bible commentaries for in-person participants' use.) After allowing sufficient time for discussion, ask someone from each small group to report highlights from their discussion. Encourage participants to note similarities and differences between the three scriptures, and what those similarities and differences may mean.

Discuss:

- What difference does getting and keeping the connection clear between John and Jesus make to Christians today?
- Hamilton suggests that John, in his attitude toward Jesus, is teaching us something about life, and what it means to be human: it is humility, celebrating the success of others, working to shine light instead of shade on others' work. When was a time you learned a lesson in humility? When are you tempted to throw shade instead of shine light on others, and how do you deal with that temptation?

CONSIDERING CONSEQUENCES OF SPEAKING TRUTH TO POWER

Recruit volunteers to read aloud Mark 6:17-29, while other participants read along silently. Discuss:

- Why did King Herod imprison John (verses 17-18)? Who do you know or know of who has suffered serious consequences for speaking up to someone in power? Have you? What happened?
- "Some would call [John's actions] mixing religion and politics," writes Hamilton (p. 125). Would you? Why or why not? What are appropriate and inappropriate ways for Christians—individually, as congregations, in denominations—to "mix" religion and politics? How do we discern the difference?

- Why do you think Herod found John's message confusing—and why did he enjoy listening to John all the same (verse 20)? Why do you think Mark includes this detail in his account of John's death?

- How do Herod's promise (verses 22-23) and his regret at keeping it (verse 26) contribute to your opinion of him? When, if ever, have you done something to avoid losing face in front of others?

- Hamilton draws parallels between the behavior and attitudes of Herod and Herodias in the first century and the way power corrupts people in today's world. How have you seen power corrupting powerful people, in history and today?

- Hamilton writes of powerful bullies that "One way or another, justice ultimately prevails" (p. 127). What do you think of this assertion? How does or how should a promise of future judgment shape what the church does and doesn't do in response to powerful bullies today?

- How is the story of John's death like and unlike the story of Jesus's death? What significance can you find in these similarities and differences?

- Hamilton says that John's death brings to his mind the question, "What am I willing to die for?" How do you answer this question? How certain are you of your answer, and why?

WITNESSING TO THE LIGHT

Recruit volunteers to read aloud John 1:1-14, while other participants read along silently. Tell participants that scholars generally identify these verses as the "prologue" to John's Gospel. Discuss:

- What claims do these verses make about who Jesus is? Which of these claims appeal to or inspire you the most? Which confuse you?

- The "Word" (Greek *logos*) was an idea familiar in first-century religion and philosophy. According to Hamilton, it refers to "God's essence, God's self-disclosure, the very logic of God" (p. 132). What modern images or metaphors, if any, would communicate John's claims about "the Word" to people today?
- What meanings and values do you associate with light and darkness? What does the image of light in darkness communicate about who Jesus is? How well do you think this image communicates John's claims in today's world, and why?
- Hamilton points out that, in his congregation's Christmas Eve worship, "we always skip" verses 6-8, prose verses about John the Baptist that seem "a jarring interruption, misplaced in the midst of this glorious poetry" (p. 132). Why do you think John the Evangelist chose to introduce John the Baptist at this point?
- Hamilton likens the mission of John to the moon, which reflects the light of the sun. What other images can you think of to describe John's mission and connection to Jesus?
- Hamilton offers his congregation's work helping refugees from Afghanistan as one example of following John the Baptist's work, testifying to the light. How is your congregation witnessing to the light this Advent and Christmas season?
- How are you, as an individual follower of Jesus, witnessing to the light? Which of these forms of witness, or what new ones, will you continue in the new year?

CLOSING YOUR SESSION: EXTENDING CHRIST'S INVITATION TO OTHERS

Read aloud from *Prepare the Way for the Lord*: "I wonder if God is calling you to be his messenger; to prepare the way of the Lord, by inviting someone to Christmas Eve worship.... We're meant to testify to the light with our actions, but also by our words in witness and invitation. Your mission, like John's, is to testify to the light (pp. 139–140).

Ask participants to think of at least one person they could invite to worship with them this Christmas season, or to some other activity in or with your congregation where they might encounter people "witnessing to the light." Invite volunteers to make public commitments to invite a specific individual.

Spend a few minutes reviewing this study series with participants, asking volunteers to talk briefly about one concrete way they believe the study has shaped their faith and practice. Thank all participants for their involvement.

Read this prayer, or one of your own, aloud:

As we celebrate your Word made flesh in Jesus Christ, O God, we dare to ask that your Word would also become flesh, in a lesser but no less real way, in each of our lives. Make us, more and more, into people who witness to your light by all we say and do. As you gave your faithful servant John, give us grace, boldness, and love to point everyone to Jesus, proclaiming, "Behold the Lamb of God!" Amen.

SING TOGETHER (OPTIONAL)

Hamilton says one of his favorite hymns is "Come, Thou Fount of Every Blessing" (Robert Robinson, 1758; https://hymnary.org/text /come_thou_fount_of_every_blessing). Sing or read together the lyrics of this hymn as your closing prayer.

OPTIONAL EXTENSIONS

- As Hamilton writes, Mandaenism or Sabianism is a religion with "about sixty thousand adherents around world that considers John the Baptist, not Jesus, to be their chief prophet" (p. 118). Encourage interested participants to research this religion, using reliable sources, and to share highlights from their research with the group after this study ends (whether informally, by email, or in some future gathering).

• In a postscript to the book, Adam Hamilton discusses the Christian concept of Judgment Day, which has its roots in both the Old and New Testaments, and the Second Advent of Jesus. This concept is known in biblical studies and theology as "eschatology," which includes both the end of history and what happens to us after we die. Spend some time as a group discussing various ideas of the end of history that they have encountered. Ultimately, we can't know when Christ will return. What is the important thing Hamilton emphasizes, recognizing this uncertainty? In what ways are you living as a people prepared for, and preparing, the way of the Lord?